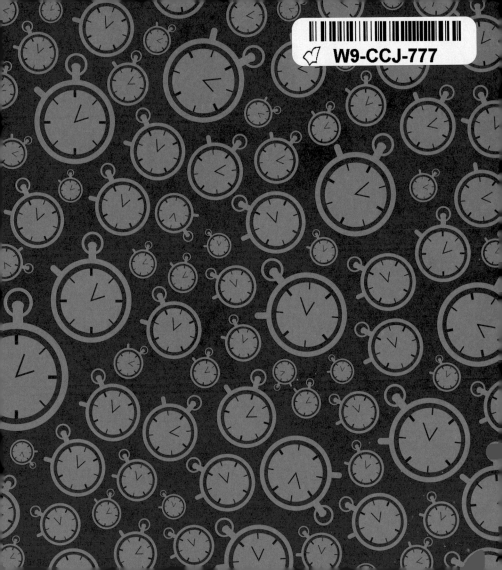

The Race

Life's Greatest Lesson

By Dee Groberg

Introduction by Mac Anderson

WARNER
Faith

New York   Boston   Nashville

The Race

Written by: Dee Groberg
Introduction by: Mac Anderson
Designed by: McMillan Associates

Warner Faith
Time Warner Book Group
1271 Avenue of the Americas, New York, NY 10020

Visit our website at www.twbookmark.com

Printed in Singapore
First Warner Faith Printing: May 2004

10 9 8 7 6 5 4 3 2 1

Library of Congress Cataloging-in-Publication Data

Groberg, Dee.
  The race: life's greatest lesson / Dee Groberg.
    p. cm.
  ISBN 0-446-53307-6
1. Failure (Psychology)—Poetry.   2. Fathers and
sons—Poetry.   3. Conduct of life—Poetry.
4. Running races—Poetry.   5. Success—Poetry.
6. Boys—Poetry.   I. Title. PS3607.R627R33 2004
811'.6—dc22

2003019184

Thank You:

Michael McMillan, whose genius and creative
vision brought this story to life.

Megan Kearney, whose creative input and tireless
effort was invaluable.

My long time friend, Peter Walts, who shared
my vision to publish this story and helped to
find the author.

My friend Vince Lombardi, Jr. for sharing the
words to "The Race" more than seven years ago.

Of course, a big thanks to the author, D.H. Groberg
who, more than twenty years ago was inspired to
capture this wonderful "life lesson" in words.

—*Mac Anderson*

To: ——————————

From: ——————————

Date: ——————————

Introduction *by Mac Anderson*

I remember the moment like it was yesterday. I had just attended a difficult board meeting at Successories that morning and was scheduled to meet our banker in the afternoon for what promised to be another challenging meeting. In short, it was a difficult time in my life. I stopped by my office before my next meeting, and sitting on top of my stack of mail was a letter from Vince Lombardi, Jr. (the son of the legendary coach) whom I had known for a few years. I opened the letter and there was a short note saying, "Mac, you're going to love this poem as much as I do. It's called 'The Race,' and to me, it teaches life's greatest lesson."

I began to read, and for the next few minutes I was mesmerized. When I finished, I had goose bumps. The words touched my heart like nothing else I had ever read. Maybe it was the timing as to what was going on in my life, but my soul was receptive and this simple story provided an "Aha!" moment. It helped to give me the courage and belief I needed to fight through the adversity I was facing.

With Successories back on track, I suddenly faced another crisis on the personal front. At fifty-four, I was diagnosed with prostate cancer. Needless to say, the "C" word gets your attention. I faced some difficult decisions about my treatment and about what I wanted to do with the rest of my life. I had been "entrepreneuring" for thirty years and decided it was time to remove myself from the day-to-day pressures of running the company and focus on more personal interests.

Therefore, while continuing to work with Successories on the creative front, I also pursued something I had always wanted to do, but never had the time—speak professionally about my entrepreneur experiences. It seems that when we pursue the things really important to us, new discoveries present themselves in profound ways. With that in mind, I've closed my presentation to corporate audiences with "The Race" for the past two years. The reaction has been amazing. I've had hundreds of people approach me afterwards, asking for a copy to share with their son, daughter, friend, or coworker who was going through a difficult period in their life. So by experiencing this reaction, I knew "The Race" conveyed a message with universal appeal, and one that touched the souls of others, like it had done for me. And I wanted to somehow share it with the rest of the world.

But there were two problems. The first was a "biggie." I had no idea who wrote it, and neither did Vince. Secondly, I knew that if I published it, it must be visually compelling to have maximum impact.

I solved the second problem first by calling a friend of mine, Michael McMillan, who is one of the top designers in the country. The first book he designed, *Rare Air*, for Michael Jordan, was a bestseller. It was a beautifully designed coffee-table book with great visual impact. However, it was his most recent book that he authored, *Paper Airplane: The Flight of Change*, that convinced me that Michael was the person who would bring "The Race" to life. We met, and after reading the poem, he agreed to be a part of the project.

The next hurdle—finding the author. It took several weeks, but another friend, Peter Walts, was persistent in his search via the Internet. After going down one blind alley after another, he finally discovered that Mr. Dee Groberg, from Salt Lake City, Utah, had written the poem more than twenty-five years ago. I called Dee and introduced myself, letting him know what an inspiration his poem had been to me and to my corporate audiences. He said that he'd had many offers to publish the work, but he wanted to present it in a special, "one-of-a-kind" format. I shared my vision of working with Michael McMillan to give readers a memorable experience, and after three or four lengthy conversations, Dee said, "Let's do it."

I have been blessed at Successories to have been involved in the creation of many products that have touched hearts and lives in a positive way. It is always a magical moment when someone writes or calls just to say, "Your products made a difference in my life."

However, of all the products I've helped to launch, there have been none that I'm more passionate about than this book. In my opinion, "The Race" does teach life's greatest lesson.

Read it! Enjoy it! Apply the lessons to your life! All I ask is that if you like it... share it with the rest of the world.

I wish you the best.

Mac Anderson
Founder, Successories

"Quit! Give up

They shout a

ou're beaten!"

he and plead.

"There's just too much against you now

This time yo

an't succeed."

And as I start to hang my head
In front of failure's face,
My downward fall is broken by
The memory of a race.

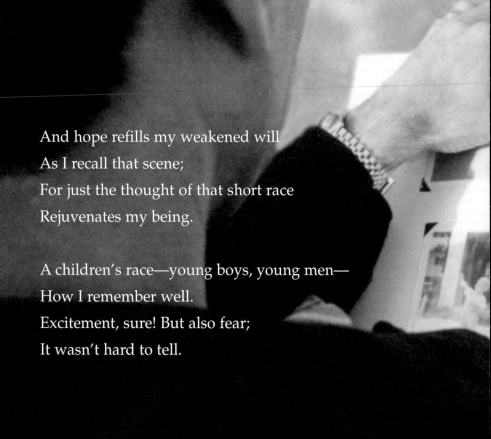

And hope refills my weakened will
As I recall that scene;
For just the thought of that short race
Rejuvenates my being.

A children's race—young boys, young men—
How I remember well.
Excitement, sure! But also fear;
It wasn't hard to tell.

They all lined up so full of hope;
Each thought to win that race.
Or tie for first, or if not that,
At least take second place.

And fathers watched from off the side
Each cheering for his son.
And each boy hoped to show his dad
That he would be the one.

The whistle blew and off they went,
Young hearts and hopes afire.
To win and be the hero there
Was each young boy's desire.

annual "back to school" race.

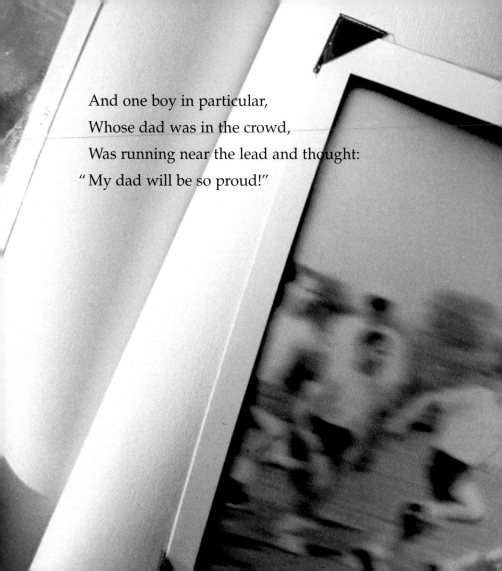

And one boy in particular,
Whose dad was in the crowd,
Was running near the lead and thought:
" My dad will be so proud!"

annual "back to school" race.

But as they sped down the field

Across a shallow dip

The little boy who thought to win Lost his step and slipped.

Trying hard to catch himself,
His hands flew out to brace,
But mid the laughter of the crowd
He fell flat on his face.

So down he fell and with him hope
He couldn't win it now—

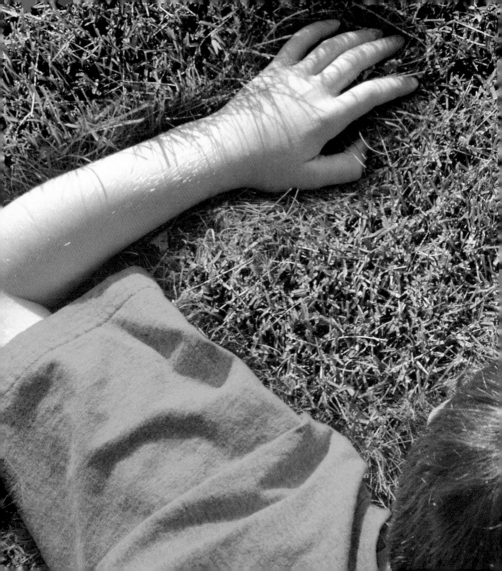

Embarrassed, sad, he only wished   To disappear some

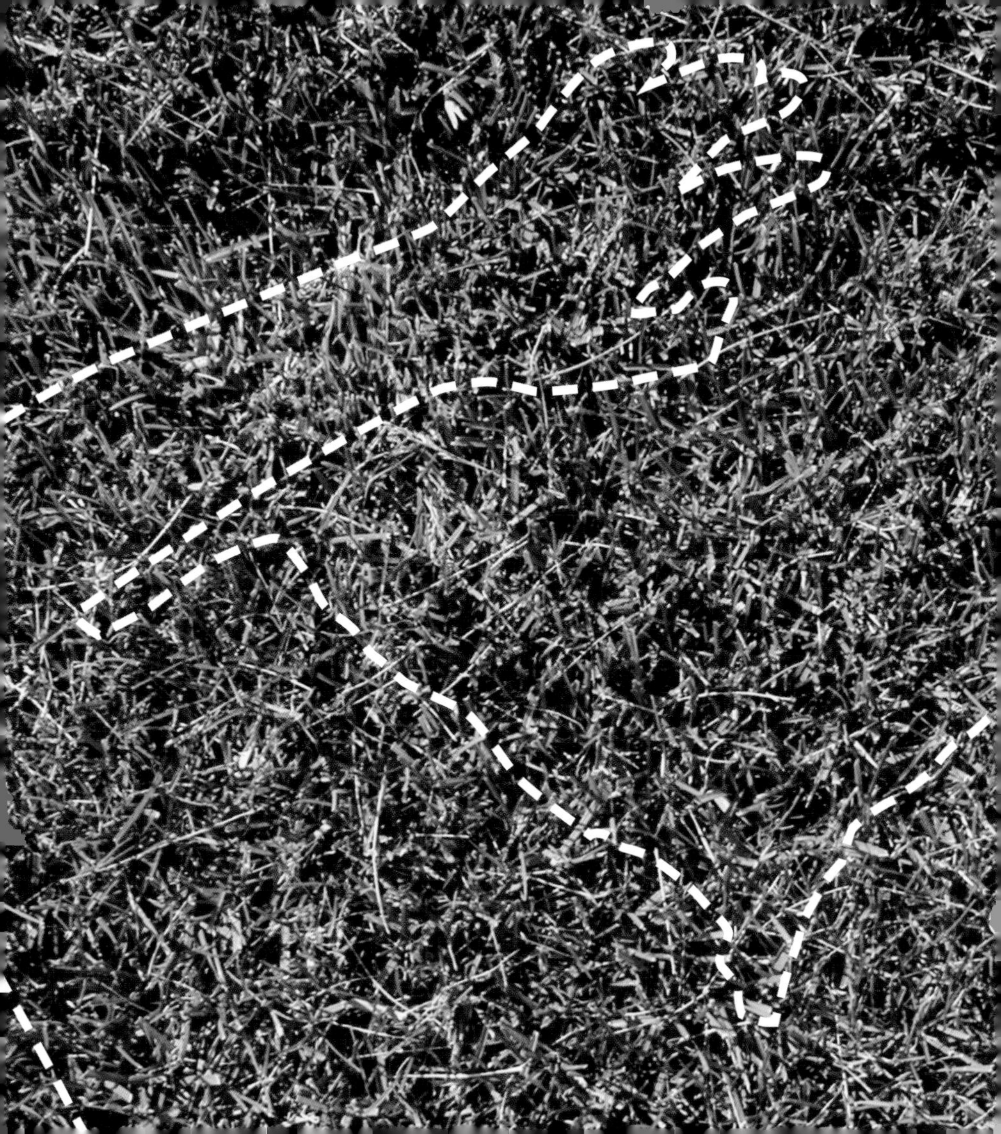

But as he fell his dad stood up,
And showed his anxious face,
Which to the boy so clearly said,
"Get up and win the race."

He quickly rose, no damage done,
Behind a bit, that's all—
And ran with all his mind and might
To make up for his fall.

So anxious to restore himself
To catch up and to win—
His mind went faster than his legs;
He slipped and fell again!

He wished then he had quit before,
With only one disgrace.
"I'm hopeless as a runner now;
I shouldn't try to race."

But in the laughing crowd he searched

And found his father's face;

That steady look which said again:

"Get up and

win the race!"

So up he jumped to try again
Ten yards behind the last—
"If I'm to gain those yards," he thought,
"I've got to move real fast."

Exerting everything he had
He regained eight or ten,
But trying so hard to catch the lead
He slipped and fell again!

Defeat! He lay there silently
A tear dropped from his eye—

" There's no sense running anymore;
Three strikes: I'm out! Why try!"

The will to rise had disappeared;

All hope had fled away;

So far behind, so error prone;

A loser all the way.

"I've lost, so what's the use," he thought,

"I'll live with my disgrace."

But then he thought about his dad
Who soon he'd have to face.

"Get up," an echo sounded low.
"Get up and take your place;
    You were not meant for failure here.
    Get up and win the race."

"With borrowed will get up," it said,

"You haven't lost at all.

For winning is no more than this:

To rise each time you fall."

So up he rose to run once more,

And with a new commit

He resolved that

or Lose

At least he wouldn't quit.

So far behind the others now,
The most he'd ever been—
Still he gave it all he had
And ran as though to win.

Three times he'd fallen, stumbling;
Three times he rose again;
Too far behind to hope to win
He still ran to the end.

They cheered the winning runn
As he crossed the line first plac
Head high, and proud, and hap
No falling, no disgrace.

But when the fallen youngster
Crossed the line last place,
The crowd gave him the greater cheer,
For finishing the race.

And even though he came in last,
With head bowed low, unproud,
You would have thought he'd won the race
To listen to the crowd.

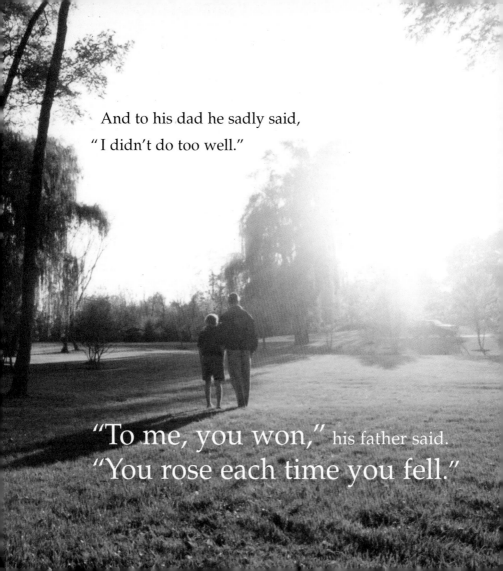

And to his dad he sadly said,
"I didn't do too well."

"To me, you won," his father said.
"You rose each time you fell."

And now when things seem dark and hard
And difficult to face,
The memory of that little boy
Helps me in my race.

For all of life is like that race,
With ups and downs and all.
And all you have to do to win,
Is rise each time you fall.

Closing Thoughts

It has been a great privilege to be involved in bringing "The Race" to life. As I had mentioned earlier, as the founder of Successories, I've launched many inspirational products but there are none that I'm more passionate about than this one. When one of life's greatest lessons is told in a memorable way, adding compelling graphics...magic happens!

Again, I would like to thank the author Dee Groberg, talented designer Michael McMillan, and Warner Books for making this project all it could be.

Because of my enthusiasm for "The Race" and my efforts in getting it published, something wonderful has happened. It seems that many of the people I've shared it with have their own favorite inspirational story or poem that they want me to read. They will bring it out of a special place in their desk, their briefcase, or their purse. Although, in some cases, worn and tattered from use they hand it to me with great pride and say, "These words have made a difference in my life. What do you think?" I've been amazed at how many great stories and poems I've seen in the past few months. So amazed in fact, that I have decided to make a concentrated effort to bring the best ones to life with other gift books like this one. So, if you have a favorite that you've written or enjoyed over the years, please submit it for consideration to:

Mac Anderson
Successories
2520 Diehl Road
Aurora, IL 60504

In closing, I hope you enjoyed "The Race" as much as I did when I read it for the first time. And if you did, read it often. It works the second, third, and tenth time almost as well as the first. We all have doubts, fears, and disappointments in our lives...and a little "shot of inspiration" can do wonders.

And one more thing...share it with those you love.

All the best,

Mac Anderson

What others are saying about THE RACE

"Once in a great while you'll read something that 'knocks your socks off.' This was one of those times."

—*Steve Dragoo, training director, ConAgra Foods*

"Every salesperson in the world should carry a copy of THE RACE in their briefcase. In five minutes you can go from feeling low to feeling great!"

—*Tom Simonian, president, Incentive Inc.*

"THE RACE is a great life lesson written and illustrated in an unforgettable way."

—*Brian Tracy, bestselling business author*

"Many, many people will be inspired by THE RACE. I had 'goose bumps' reading it."

—*Mike Singletary, Hall of Fame linebacker, coach and motivational speaker*

Dr. D. H. (Dee) Groberg is founding vice president of the International Covey Leadership Center. He has presented to a wide variety of audiences in the United States and throughout the world. Dee speaks several languages and has degrees in Asian studies (B.S.), applied linguistics (M.A.), and organizational and instructional science (Ph.D.). He has participated as a guest lecturer and educator at many international conferences on such topics as productivity, quality and training. Recently, Dr. Groberg was the keynote speaker at the National Quality Association Conference of the former U.S.S.R. in Voronezh, Russia.

Dee and his wife, Sharon, have six children. He enjoys reading, writing, poetry, music, traveling, swimming, skiing, scuba diving...and time with his family.

Mac Anderson is the founder of Successories, Inc., the leader in designing and marketing products for motivation and recognition. Successories, however, is not the first success story for Mac Anderson. He was also the founder and CEO of McCord Travel, the largest travel company in the Midwest, and part-owner/VP of sales and marketing for Orval Kent Food Company, the country's largest manufacturer of prepared salads. Mac's accomplishments in these three unrelated industries provide some insight into his passion and leadership skills.

Mac brings the same passion to his speaking and writing. He speaks to many corporate audiences on a variety of topics, including leadership, motivation and team building. He has written two books, *The Nature of Success* and *The Power of Attitude*, and has coauthored *To a Child, Love is Spelled T-I-M-E*.

For more information, please visit **www.macanderson.com**.